MW01677995

A GUIDE TO BOOK PRINTING AND SELF-PUBLISHING

Book Printing & Self-Publishing

GORHAM PRINTING
A GREAT LOOK FOR YOUR SHORT-RUN BOOK

PRINTED & PUBLISHED BY GORHAM PRINTING • 2002

Welcome to GORHAM PRINTING

A GREAT LOOK FOR YOUR SHORT-RUN BOOK

Having your book printed can be a life-fulfilling endeavor and a time to experience great pride and accomplishment. Gorham Printing is dedicated to making your book the best it can be.

This guide is designed to introduce you to the necessary preparations, technical printing details and key design decisions required for a successful transformation of your manuscript into a book.

We are a Pacific Northwest book printer specializing in the design and printing of self-published books. Our forté is the ability to print books in very short print runs—from as few as 25 copies to as many as 3,000—and in doing so, create a great look for your short-run book. Our shelves are filled with examples of our work, with subjects that include fiction, nonfiction, religious, spiritual, historical, self-help, remembrances, manuals, how-to guides, genealogies, family histories, adventure, and more!

First-time authors as well as veteran writers have come to depend upon our hallmark qualities: careful attention to detail, customized design work, top-notch printing skills, and true, one-on-one, personal service. Just as you take pride as an author, we take equal pride in the books that we print.

If you should have any questions, concerns, or wish to have a price quote for your book project, don't hesitate to contact us. We look forward to hearing from you.

VISIT US ONLINE AT
www.
gorhamprinting.com

OR EMAIL US AT
info@
gorhamprinting.com

CALL US AT
(800) 837-0970 *or*
(360) 273-0970

FAX US AT
(360) 273-8679

MAIL US AT
334 Harris Road
Rochester, WA 98579

HOURS
8:30-5:00
Monday-Friday

Kurt Gorham, Editor
Illustrations by Kathy Campbell

Printed and published by
GORHAM PRINTING
Rochester, Washington

Third Edition, First Printing

Printed in the United States of America

ISBN 0-9676922-1-0
Library of Congress Control Number: 00-190042

CONTENTS

DECISIONS AFFECTING COST

Decisions about quantities, book size & paper stock, cover and page design, photographs & art, printing, bindings and price list

Decisions, decisions...

Refer to the price lists starting on page 14 to determine the cost of your book project.

Quantity & Cost

One of the first questions you might ask yourself is, "How much will it cost to print my book?" The answer depends largely on how many copies you want. In general, the more copies printed, the less each one costs. That is because setup expenses are the same whether we print one book or thousands. Therefore, if the cost of setup is spread over many books, the cost per book will be lower.

What size should it be?

Almost any size is possible, but some sizes are more efficient and less expensive. Our standard sizes are 5¼ x 8¼″, 5½ x 8½″, 6 x 9″ and 8¼ x 10¾″, 8½ x 11″. These sizes are the most economical since they minimize paper waste.

To get the most for your money, keep your book to our standard trim sizes. For example, if you want a 7 x 9″ book rather than a 6 x 9″, it would be priced at the 8½ x 11″ size. We print in 16–page signatures, so your total page count needs to be divisible by 16.

The size of your book is sometimes dependent on its subject matter. 5½ x 8½″ or 6 x 9″ are the sizes most often used. A short column width makes the book very readable, easy to handle, ship and display. A 6 x 9″ book offers more space for photos, but for books with many photos, maps or illustrations, 8½ x 11″ is a better size format.

What kind of paper is used for the text?

Our "house sheet" is 60# white Georgia Pacific Spectrum offset for text, which we order in large quantities, resulting in savings for you. We can also special-order other colors and weights upon request.

What kind of paper is used for the cover?

For softcover books we use white 10 point C1S, which is a heavy weight stock coated on one side (C1S). Other papers are also available; check with us for details. If the book is hardcover, the cover can be foil stamped or printed.

How is the cover protected?

The covers are laminated with a plastic film. The film protects the ink from scuffing and can give the book either a glossy or matte finish.

How long does it take? If your book is already designed and ready for printing, it takes approximately 4-6 weeks to complete. If formatting and designing is required, allow an additional 2-6 weeks.

Book Design

People *do* judge a book by its cover. We can design a cover to be printed in four colors (full color) or in one, two or three spot colors, depending upon your budget and market. Often two colors will give you a professional look for less money. However, you may want to consider a full-color cover, which costs more, but gives more flexibility and design options. Having designed a wide variety of covers, we are adept at creating just the right look for your audience.

We will work with you to create a cover you like, discussing what you have in mind and providing you with mock-ups for approval. We charge between $300.00 and $400.00 (not including color separations or complex artwork) to completely design your cover, including typesetting, design and proofs.

Text Design

Designing a readable and attractive page of text is a subtle art. Let us use our expertise to correctly determine your typestyle, point size, leading, and line lengths to provide optimum impact for your text layout, front matter, chapter heads and other design details. *See Additional Design Information beginning on page 25.*

If your text pages are saved on a computer disk in a word processing program such as Word or Wordperfect, we will import your file into Adobe PageMaker or Adobe InDesign, a page layout program. We provide this service for approximately $2.25 per page.

As an alternative, for those who would like a good look for less, we offer template book design for both the text and cover on 6 x 9″ books. From classic, time-proven designs, to a more subject-specific look for your book, these templates will give your book a professional look for less money. Check our website for more details.

If you are submitting text for us to format, check page 42 for more details on what to send.
If you are submitting text ready for trouble-free output, please check page 44 for more details.

Photographs & Art

A printing press simulates shades of gray by printing larger or smaller dots. The larger dots represent shadow areas while the smaller dots represent highlight areas. The technique of making a photo ready to be printed is known as making a *halftone.*

In order to print photos in your book a *halftone* must be made of the original photograph. We charge $9.00 per photo to scan and place photos within the text of your book. If your photos are already scanned, we can optimize and place them within the text for $5.00.

When submitting photos an organized method is necessary for us to know where each photo and caption belongs in the book. Numbering the photo and caption to its corresponding page number is one easy method. Quality of the printed photo will depend upon the quality of the original. We can do minor repairs to photos, but if they are blurry or seriously damaged, we will not be able to achieve a quality outcome. Halftones made from previously printed photos give marginal results. (Remember to check copyright restrictions.) Good quality color photos can be easily reproduced as black and white. Photos can also be reduced and enlarged as needed.

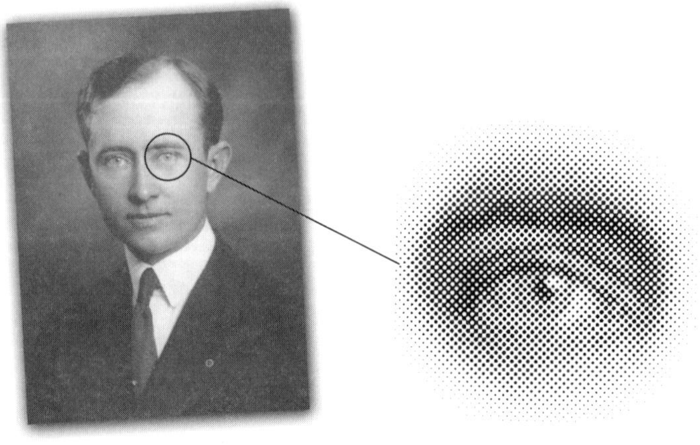

Bindings

Perfect Binding (softcover)

Often called a "paperback" book, this type of book is bound using hot flexible glue. A book must have a minimum of 64 pages to be bound this way. As an example, this book is perfect bound.

Casebinding (hardcover)

The most durable binding method. The page signatures are sewn (smyth sewn) together, reinforced and attached to the hardcover, which can be covered with non-woven book material, bookcloth, imitation leather or a printed and laminated paper.

A "split run" is when a run of books is partially perfect bound and partially casebound. Hardcover books can also be part of a "limited edition" and can include colored endsheets and ribbon markers.

Plastic Spiral Binding

A ideal binding for books that must open and lie flat, such as cookbooks, workbooks, teachers' guides or manuals.

Printing Options

We offer two printing methods for your book.

Offset Printed Books

This is the best choice for run lengths of 300 books or more. Our prices for this printing method begin on page 15.

Digitally Printed Books

Our newest method offers some real cost advantages for very short print runs, or 25-300 books. In the past, printing a short run of books, say 100, was very expensive per book. After much research we have come up with a good quality solution.

Our digitally printed books offer many features:

- full color covers on 10 point laminated cover stock
- 60# white offset paper stock for the text pages
- Five finished trim sizes to choose from; 5¼ x 8¼″, 5½ x 8½″, 6 x 9″, 8¼ x 10¾″ and 8½ x 11″.

These features are available for quantities as low as 25 books! Combine the quality of these digitally printed books with our expertise in layout and design to give you "a great look for your short-run book." Our prices for digitally printed books begin on page 17.

Overruns

When your book is printed, an overrun may occur as we print a higher than ordered quantity to compensate for spoilage that may occur in the various printing and binding processes. Overruns are priced per book based on the quoted price minus layout and design costs.

Offset Printed Books

PRICES INCLUDE

- Text printed in black ink on 60# white paper
- Cover printed in two colors on 10 point white C1S (coated one side) stock
- Gloss lamination on the cover
- Aluminum plates
- Perfect binding
- Trim on 3 sides
- Delivery (within 60 miles of our plant)

All prices are based on manufacturing books from a disk ready for trouble-free output. Prices do not include formatting from computer disk, cover design or illustration. Books with many photos, line art, etc., may result in additional charges. For other quantities, either in number of pages or number of books, please call for quotations.

5½ x 8½″

All prices refer to price per book

	QUANTITY					
PAGES	100	250	500	1,000	2,000	3,000
64	6.91	3.41	2.25	1.66	1.37	1.26
80	7.63	3.75	2.47	1.82	1.49	1.37
96	8.44	4.15	2.73	2.01	1.65	1.52
112	9.21	4.54	2.99	2.21	1.81	1.67
128	9.94	4.89	3.22	2.37	1.95	1.79
144	10.73	5.32	3.51	2.60	2.14	1.96
160	11.46	5.67	3.74	2.76	2.25	2.08
176	12.22	6.07	3.99	2.96	2.42	2.23
192	13.02	6.43	4.24	3.14	2.56	2.37
208	13.75	6.79	4.48	3.31	2.70	2.45
224	14.53	7.21	4.74	3.52	2.87	2.61
240	15.26	7.55	4.98	3.68	3.00	2.73
256	16.01	7.92	5.22	3.86	3.15	2.85
272	16.72	8.34	5.53	4.12	3.37	3.07
288	17.49	8.69	5.75	4.28	3.50	3.19
304	18.25	9.08	6.01	4.44	3.60	3.33
320	19.00	9.47	6.28	4.64	3.77	3.49
336	19.76	9.84	6.53	4.83	3.92	3.63
352	20.47	10.21	6.75	5.00	4.05	3.74
368	21.22	10.58	7.01	5.18	4.19	3.88
384	21.99	10.92	7.23	5.34	4.32	3.99
400	22.74	11.31	7.48	5.52	4.47	4.13

PRICES EFFECTIVE 1/2000, SUBJECT TO CHANGE WITHOUT NOTICE

6 x 9″

All prices refer to price per book

PAGES	QUANTITY 100	250	500	1,000	2,000	3,000
64	7.14	3.55	2.34	1.74	1.43	1.33
80	7.93	3.93	2.59	1.92	1.58	1.46
96	8.74	4.34	2.87	2.13	1.76	1.63
112	9.56	4.78	3.16	2.35	1.95	1.76
128	10.42	5.16	3.42	2.54	2.09	1.90
144	11.26	5.61	3.73	2.78	2.30	2.08
160	12.05	5.99	3.98	2.96	2.40	2.22
176	12.86	6.42	4.27	3.19	2.57	2.38
192	13.66	6.82	4.53	3.38	2.73	2.53
208	14.46	7.21	4.79	3.58	2.88	2.62
224	15.29	7.66	5.08	3.80	3.08	2.80
240	16.14	8.05	5.34	3.99	3.22	2.92
256	16.94	8.44	5.62	4.19	3.38	3.07
272	17.71	8.90	5.94	4.46	3.62	3.29
288	18.62	9.33	6.22	4.66	3.77	3.43
304	19.30	9.69	6.47	4.75	3.86	3.58
320	20.11	10.10	6.76	4.97	4.04	3.74
336	20.92	10.54	7.03	5.18	4.21	3.90
352	21.69	10.91	7.29	5.35	4.35	4.03
368	22.56	11.31	7.57	5.55	4.51	4.17
384	23.34	11.72	7.81	5.73	4.65	4.30
400	24.14	12.12	8.09	5.93	4.81	4.45

PRICES EFFECTIVE 1/2000, SUBJECT TO CHANGE WITHOUT NOTICE

8½ x 11″

All prices refer to price per book

PAGES	QUANTITY 100	250	500	1,000	2,000	3,000
64	9.81	4.96	3.34	2.52	2.09	1.93
80	11.23	5.67	3.81	2.85	2.35	2.18
96	12.67	6.38	4.27	3.19	2.61	2.43
112	14.13	7.13	4.77	3.57	2.92	2.71
128	15.57	7.82	5.23	3.90	3.18	2.95
144	16.93	8.55	5.71	4.29	3.52	3.27
160	18.36	9.24	6.16	4.57	3.78	3.52
176	19.79	9.99	6.65	4.93	4.08	3.79
192	21.22	10.68	7.11	5.26	4.35	4.04
208	22.64	11.40	7.58	5.60	4.63	4.30
224	24.10	12.13	8.06	5.96	4.93	4.58
240	25.53	12.82	8.51	6.29	5.20	4.82
256	26.95	13.55	9.00	6.64	5.49	5.09
272	28.36	14.22	9.49	7.01	5.81	5.39
288	29.75	14.90	9.83	7.34	6.07	5.63
304	31.19	15.61	10.30	7.69	6.36	5.89
320	32.65	16.36	10.80	8.07	6.68	6.19
336	34.12	17.17	11.30	8.45	7.00	6.49
352	35.47	17.83	11.70	8.73	7.22	6.69
368	36.91	18.48	12.16	9.07	7.49	6.95
384	38.26	19.16	12.62	9.42	7.79	7.22
400	39.78	19.94	13.16	9.84	8.14	7.55

PRICES EFFECTIVE 1/2000, SUBJECT TO CHANGE WITHOUT NOTICE

Digitally Printed Books

PRICES INCLUDE

- Text printed in black ink on 60# white paper
- Full color cover on 10 point white C1S (coated one side) stock
- Gloss lamination on the cover
- Perfect binding
- Trim on 3 sides

All prices are based on manufacturing books from a disk ready for trouble-free output. Prices do not include formatting from computer disk, cover design or illustration. Books with many photos, line art, etc., may result in additional charges. For other quantities, either in number of pages or number of books, please call for quotations.

5¼ x 8¼″

All prices refer to price per book

	QUANTITY					
PAGES	25	50	100	150	200	250
64	6.22	4.61	3.80	3.54	3.41	3.33
80	6.48	4.87	4.06	3.80	3.66	3.59
96	6.74	5.12	4.31	4.06	3.92	3.84
112	7.02	5.39	4.58	4.32	4.18	4.11
128	7.31	5.68	4.87	4.61	4.47	4.40
144	7.57	5.94	5.12	4.87	4.73	4.65
160	7.86	6.23	5.41	5.16	5.02	4.94
176	8.11	6.48	5.67	5.41	5.27	5.20
192	8.37	6.74	5.92	5.67	5.53	5.46
208	8.69	7.04	6.22	5.97	5.82	5.75
224	8.94	7.30	6.48	6.22	6.08	6.01
240	9.20	7.56	6.73	6.48	6.34	6.27
256	9.49	7.84	7.02	6.77	6.63	6.55
272	9.74	8.10	7.28	7.02	6.88	6.81
288	10.00	8.36	7.53	7.28	7.14	7.07
304	10.33	8.67	7.84	7.59	7.44	7.37
320	10.59	8.93	8.10	7.85	7.70	7.63
336	10.86	9.19	8.36	8.11	7.96	7.89
352	11.12	9.45	8.61	8.37	8.22	8.15
368	11.38	9.71	8.87	8.62	8.48	8.41
384	11.63	9.96	9.13	8.88	8.73	8.66
400	11.93	10.26	9.43	9.18	9.03	8.96

PRICES EFFECTIVE 1/2000, SUBJECT TO CHANGE WITHOUT NOTICE

5½ x 8½″

All prices refer to price per book

PAGES	QUANTITY 25	50	100	150	200	250
64	6.58	4.97	4.16	3.90	3.76	3.69
80	6.93	5.31	4.51	4.25	4.11	4.04
96	7.28	5.66	4.85	4.60	4.46	4.38
112	7.65	6.02	5.21	4.95	4.81	4.74
128	8.03	6.40	5.58	5.33	5.19	5.12
144	8.38	6.75	5.93	5.68	5.54	5.46
160	8.75	7.12	6.31	6.05	5.91	5.84
176	9.10	7.47	6.66	6.40	6.26	6.19
192	9.45	7.82	7.00	6.75	6.61	6.53
208	9.85	8.21	7.39	7.13	6.99	6.92
224	10.20	8.56	7.73	7.48	7.34	7.27
240	10.55	8.90	8.08	7.83	7.68	7.61
256	10.92	9.28	8.46	8.20	8.06	7.99
272	11.27	9.63	8.80	8.55	8.41	8.34
288	11.62	9.97	9.15	8.90	8.76	8.68
304	12.03	10.37	9.54	9.29	9.15	9.08
320	12.38	10.72	9.89	9.64	9.50	9.43
336	12.75	11.08	10.24	9.99	9.85	9.78
352	13.10	11.43	10.59	10.34	10.20	10.13
368	13.44	11.77	10.94	10.69	10.54	10.47
384	13.79	12.12	11.28	11.04	10.89	10.82
400	14.18	12.51	11.67	11.42	11.28	11.21

PRICES EFFECTIVE 1/2000, SUBJECT TO CHANGE WITHOUT NOTICE

6 x 9″

All prices refer to price per book

PAGES	QUANTITY 25	50	100	150	200	250
64	6.72	5.10	4.29	4.04	3.90	3.82
80	7.10	5.48	4.67	4.42	4.28	4.20
96	7.48	5.86	5.05	4.80	4.66	4.58
112	7.89	6.26	5.44	5.19	5.04	4.97
128	8.30	6.67	5.85	5.59	5.45	5.38
144	8.68	7.05	6.23	5.97	5.83	5.76
160	9.09	7.46	6.64	6.38	6.24	6.17
176	9.47	7.84	7.02	6.76	6.62	6.55
192	9.85	8.21	7.40	7.14	7.00	6.93
208	10.29	8.64	7.81	7.56	7.42	7.35
224	10.67	9.02	8.19	7.94	7.80	7.73
240	11.05	9.40	8.57	8.32	8.18	8.11
256	11.46	9.81	8.98	8.73	8.59	8.52
272	11.84	10.19	9.36	9.11	8.97	8.90
288	12.22	10.57	9.74	9.49	9.35	9.28
304	12.67	11.00	10.17	9.92	9.77	9.70
320	13.05	11.38	10.55	10.30	10.15	10.08
336	13.45	11.77	10.93	10.69	10.54	10.47
352	13.83	12.15	11.31	11.07	10.92	10.85
368	14.21	12.53	11.69	11.45	11.30	11.23
384	14.58	12.91	12.07	11.82	11.68	11.61
400	15.00	13.33	12.49	12.24	12.10	12.03

PRICES EFFECTIVE 1/2000, SUBJECT TO CHANGE WITHOUT NOTICE

8¼ x 10¾″

All prices refer to price per book

PAGES	QUANTITY 25	50	100	150	200	250
64	7.33	5.68	4.86	4.61	4.46	4.39
80	7.85	6.20	5.37	5.12	4.98	4.90
96	8.36	6.71	5.89	5.63	5.49	5.42
112	8.93	7.25	6.41	6.17	6.02	5.95
128	9.48	7.80	6.96	6.71	6.57	6.50
144	10.00	8.32	7.48	7.23	7.08	7.01
160	10.54	8.86	8.02	7.78	7.63	7.56
176	11.06	9.38	8.54	8.29	8.14	8.07
192	11.57	9.89	9.05	8.80	8.66	8.59
208	12.18	10.47	9.61	9.37	9.22	9.15
224	12.69	10.98	10.13	9.89	9.73	9.67
240	13.21	11.50	10.64	10.40	10.25	10.18
256	13.75	12.04	11.19	10.95	10.79	10.73
272	14.27	12.56	11.70	11.46	11.31	11.24
288	14.78	13.07	12.22	11.97	11.82	11.76
304	15.40	13.66	12.79	12.55	12.39	12.33
320	15.91	14.17	13.30	13.07	12.91	12.85
336	16.49	14.72	13.83	13.60	13.44	13.38
352	17.00	15.23	14.35	14.12	13.95	13.89
368	17.52	15.75	14.86	14.63	14.47	14.41
384	18.03	16.26	15.37	15.14	14.98	14.92
400	18.59	16.82	15.93	15.70	15.54	15.48

PRICES EFFECTIVE 1/2000, SUBJECT TO CHANGE WITHOUT NOTICE

8½ x 11″

All prices refer to price per book

PAGES	QUANTITY 25	50	100	150	200	250
64	8.05	6.40	5.58	5.32	5.18	5.11
80	8.74	7.09	6.27	6.02	5.87	5.80
96	9.44	7.79	6.96	6.71	6.57	6.50
112	10.19	8.51	7.67	7.42	7.28	7.21
128	10.92	9.24	8.40	8.15	8.00	7.93
144	11.61	9.93	9.09	8.85	8.70	8.63
160	12.34	10.66	9.82	9.57	9.42	9.35
176	13.03	11.35	10.51	10.27	10.12	10.05
192	13.73	12.05	11.21	10.96	10.81	10.74
208	14.51	12.80	11.95	11.71	11.55	11.49
224	15.21	13.50	12.64	12.40	12.25	12.18
240	15.90	14.19	13.33	13.09	12.94	12.87
256	16.63	14.92	14.06	13.82	13.67	13.60
272	17.32	15.61	14.75	14.51	14.36	14.29
288	18.01	16.30	15.45	15.21	15.05	14.99
304	18.81	17.07	16.20	15.96	15.81	15.74
320	19.50	17.76	16.89	16.66	16.50	16.44
336	20.26	18.49	17.60	17.37	17.21	17.15
352	20.95	19.18	18.30	18.07	17.90	17.84
368	21.65	19.88	18.99	18.76	18.60	18.54
384	22.34	20.57	19.68	19.45	19.29	19.23
400	23.08	21.31	20.42	20.19	20.03	19.97

PRICES EFFECTIVE 1/2000, SUBJECT TO CHANGE WITHOUT NOTICE

Packaging and Shipping

After your book has been completed, it is packed for shipping. We use 8½ x 11 x 12″ or 9 x 12 x 12″ boxes. See the chart below to determine the approximate weight of each box. The box weight varies depending upon the number of pages and book dimensions. Our carrier of choice is United Parcel Service.

Approximate count per carton

PAGES	5¼ x 8¼″ or 5½ x 8½″	6 x 9″	8¼ x 10¾″ or 8½ x 11″
64	142	150	71
96	100	102	50
128	78	78	39
160	62	66	31
192	54	56	27
240	42	46	21
288	36	38	18
320	32	34	16
352	30	32	15
384	26	28	13

BOOK IDENTIFICATION NUMBERS

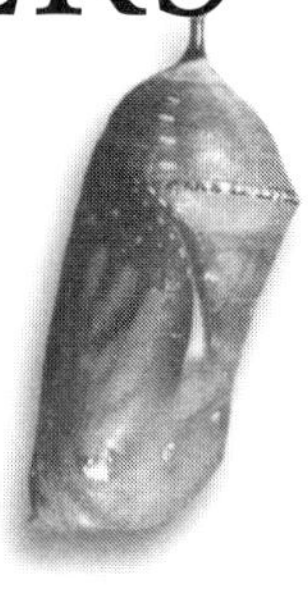

Getting a copyright, submitting your book to libraries, making your book available to bookstores

Copyright

HOTLINE
(202) 707-3000

FAX ON DEMAND
(202) 707-2600

INTERNET
http://lcweb.loc.gov/loc/infopub/publish.html

Getting a copyright

All original written works should be copyrighted. To copyright your book, place a notice on the copyright page. Either the word *copyright* and/or the © symbol must appear along with the year of first publication and the name of the copyright owner (see example).

Copyright © 2002
Bill Shakespeare
All rights reserved.

You may then elaborate on the *all rights reserved* phrase if you wish. Check other books for accepted variations.

After your book is printed, you may register your copyright by sending the following items to the U.S. Copyright Office: Form TX, a $30 fee and two copies of your book (one if it is not for sale).

For information and Form TX, request **Information Packet 109** from the *Copyright Hotline.* This phone number has recorded information available 24 hours a day, 7 days a week and information specialists are on duty from 8:30 a.m. to 5:00 p.m. EST, Monday–Friday. Information on ISBN numbers and Library of Congress Control Numbers can also be obtained from this information hotline. You can also have the appropriate forms faxed to you from the *Fax-On-Demand Line* or go to the Internet website.

Submitting your book to libraries

These numbers are issued prior to publication, and are reserved for books intended for distribution to libraries. The number is called the Preassigned Card Number (PCN) and may be requested by submitting a one-page application to the Library of Congress. The number is then printed on the copyright page of your book, preceded by the phrase, *Library of Congress Control Number.* Once the book is published, one complimentary copy is sent to the Library of Congress. (This is in addition to the two copies required by the Copyright Office.)

There are no fees for participating in the PCN program. If you believe your work would be appropriate for libraries, request a PCN. Participation sometimes results in orders for your book from sources who would not have known about it otherwise. For more information, guidelines about what books qualify, instructions and PCN forms, call Cataloging in Publications 8:30 a.m. to 5:00 p.m. EST, Monday–Friday. Or you may write to the Cataloging in Publications Division or check out their website.

Library of Congress Control Number

PHONE

(202) 707-6346

WRITE

Cataloging in
Publications Div.
Library of Congress
Washington, D.C.
20540-4320

INTERNET

http://pcn.loc.gov/pcn

ISBN

PHONE

(908) 665-6770

WRITE

ISBN Agency
R.R. Bowker
630 Central Avenue
New Providence, NJ
07974

INTERNET

http://www.isbn.org/standards/home/isbn/us/index.asp

Selling your book in the bookstores

If you plan to sell your book in a bookstore, you will probably want to obtain an ISBN (International Standard Book Number). Your ISBN in combination with a bar code is used by bookstores to order and track titles. If requested, we can provide a bar code of your number for $15.00.

R.R. Bowker Company issues these numbers, which they also publish in a reference manual *Books In Print.* The current fee is $225.00 for a block of 10 numbers. Like the Library of Congress Control Number, the ISBN must be obtained prior to publication. It usually takes about three weeks to receive your number(s). For information and instructions on how to obtain an ISBN, write or call R.R. Bowker. Information and forms can also be found on their website.

Visit our website, *gorhamprinting.com* for links and information on all book registration numbers. You can also obtain forms quickly and easily by requesting them online.

Selling your book online

Marketing a book has been made easier by the Internet. In addition to selling your book locally, you can make it available globally. The popularity of online booksellers such as *Amazon.com* and *Barnes&Noble.com* is growing steadily—many people like the ease and convenience of shopping online as well as the quick availability of a variety of titles. As another option, you can also design your own website to sell your book.

PAGE LAYOUT

Styles and suggestions for the body text, and the front and back matter of your book.

The following pages are included to provide suggestions for the design and order of the front and back matter of the book as well as the chapter heading design.

If you plan to set up text pages or your book cover yourself, check Appendix A starting on page 42 for more information about submitting your materials.

The Body Text

Choosing a Typeface

Traditionally, typefaces for books have *serifs* on their letterforms. Serifs are the strokes that project from the top or bottom of the main stroke of the letter. They assist readability by keeping the reader's eye flowing horizontally across the words. Although typefaces without serifs *(sans serif)* are increasingly popular, they are not comfortable for reading an extended amount of type as in books.

The tone or feeling of the typeface is of utmost importance. Although somewhat subjectively, most typefaces exude an impression, which, if used with complementary subject matter can enhance the mood of the writing.

"First and foremost, the forms of the letters themselves contribute much to legibility or its opposite."

—Jan Tschichold
The Form of the Book

Headers and Page Numbers

Headers at the top of each page or footers at the bottom of each page are a design option. They are not necessary in every case; for novels and poetry books a simple page number is sufficient. But they are beneficial in reference books, cookbooks and manuals because they help readers navigate their way around the different sections and chapters. Traditionally, the author's name appears on the left and the book's title on the right.

It is best to set headers as small caps with wide letterspacing in a heavy version of the body text typeface. Headers should be set at 8 or 9 points, depending upon the typeface. Headers are usually best aligned to the outside top margin of every page, with the page number on the extreme outside (there should be at least .2 inches between the number and the header).

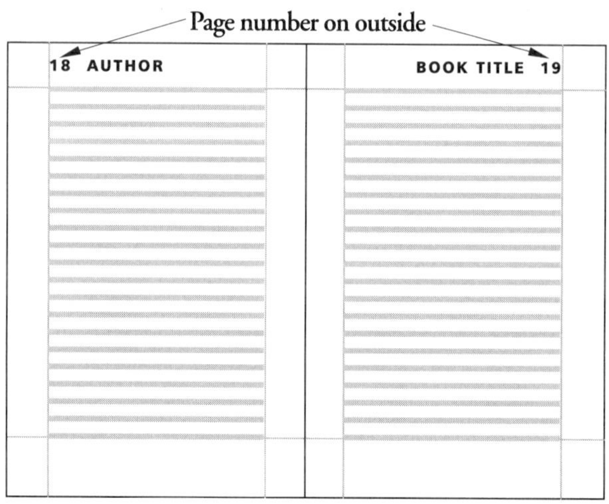

Footnotes

Footnotes should appear at the bottom of the page with their corresponding number and should be within the text block boundary. They are usually set two point sizes smaller than the body text; 8 point type on 9 point leading is a good rule of thumb. There should be about .25 of an inch of space between the top of the footnote and the body text. The footnote should always be set flush left and justified only when extremely long (6 lines or more).

Footnotes are often set with a .5 point line rule over them to distinguish them from the body text. The line should always span the column. If no line is used, the text of the footnote can be italicized to distinguish it from the body text. This should be avoided if possible because often there are italicized references in the footnote that would then have to be *un*-italicized to set *them* apart.

The number of the footnote should be superscripted, but care should be taken that it does not get too small for readability.[1]

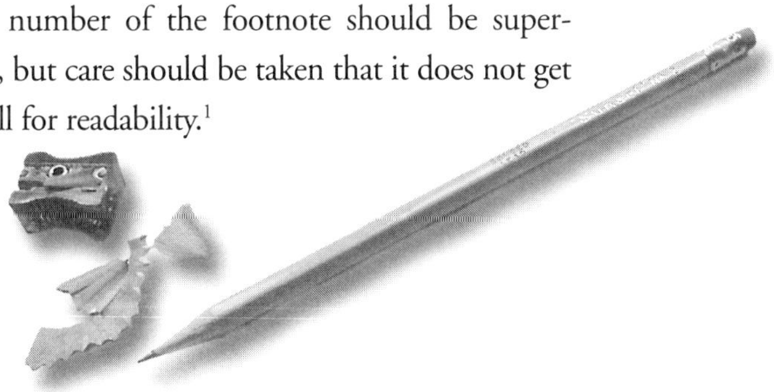

---

[1] This is an example of a good way to set the type of a footnote.

Chapter Headline Arrangement

The first page of every chapter usually contains a chapter number and headline at the top and a page number at the bottom. There are numerous design approaches one can take for these pages, which often depend upon the book's subject matter. For example, a headline for a book with a serious subject matter would be better set with everything flush left, while fiction and personal-history books look more "friendly" with chapter numbers and headlines centered. Some suggested designs we offer are as follows:

CHAPTER ONE

Headline

The typeface chosen for a book is perhaps the most important aspect of the whole design. Each typeface will convey a particular mood to the writing, unconsciously supporting the feelings invoked by the words. In this computer age of thousands of typefaces produced by many manufacturers, with trendy new faces designed every day, those that reign have proven themselves over years of typesetting use.

Readability is paramount—the spaces between letters, words and lines of type all assist or inhibit comfortable legibility. As Jan Tschichold so wisely stated: "Perfect typography depends on perfect harmony between all of its elements." This harmony is achieved by careful observation of the parts *and* the whole. A book that is improperly set can annoy the reader, in turn destroying the author's intended message, but a well-designed page will invite your eyes to read without distraction.

The typeface chosen for a book is perhaps the most important aspect of the whole design. Each typeface will convey a particular mood to the writing, unconsciously supporting the feelings invoked by the words. In this computer age of thousands of typefaces produced by many manufacturers, with trendy new faces designed every day, those that reign have proven themselves over years of typesetting use.

Readability is paramount—the spaces between letters, words and lines of type all assist or inhibit comfortable legibility. As Jan Tschichold so wisely

12

STYLE 1—*All flush left*

CHAPTER ONE

Headline

The typeface chosen for a book is perhaps the most important aspect of the whole design. Each typeface will convey a particular mood to the writing, unconsciously supporting the feelings invoked by the words. In this computer age of thousands of typefaces produced by many manufacturers, with trendy new faces designed every day, those that reign have proven themselves over years of typesetting use.

Readability is paramount—the spaces between letters, words and lines of type all assist or inhibit comfortable legibility. As Jan Tschichold so wisely stated: "Perfect typography depends on perfect harmony between all of its elements." This harmony is achieved by careful observation of the parts *and* the whole. A book that is improperly set can annoy the reader, in turn destroying the author's intended message, but a well-designed page will invite your eyes to read without distraction.

The typeface chosen for a book is perhaps the most important aspect of the whole design. Each typeface will convey a particular mood to the writing, unconsciously supporting the feelings invoked by the words. In this computer age of thousands of typefaces produced by many manufacturers, with trendy new faces designed every day, those that reign have proven themselves over years of typesetting use.

Readability is paramount—the spaces between letters, words and lines of type all assist or inhibit comfortable legibility. As Jan Tschichold so wisely

12

STYLE 2—*All centered*

CHAPTER ONE

Headline

The typeface chosen for a book is perhaps the most important aspect of the whole design. Each typeface will convey a particular mood to the writing, unconsciously supporting the feelings invoked by the words. In this computer age of thousands of typefaces produced by many manufacturers, with trendy new faces designed every day, those that reign have proven themselves over years of typesetting use.

Readability is paramount—the spaces between letters, words and lines of type all assist or inhibit comfortable legibility. As Jan Tschichold so wisely stated: "Perfect typography depends on perfect harmony between all of its elements." This harmony is achieved by careful observation of the parts *and* the whole. A book that is improperly set can annoy the reader, in turn destroying the author's intended message, but a well-designed page will invite your eyes to read without distraction.

The typeface chosen for a book is perhaps the most important aspect of the whole design. Each typeface will convey a particular mood to the writing, unconsciously supporting the feelings invoked by the words. In this computer age of thousands of typefaces produced by many manufacturers, with trendy new faces designed every day, those that reign have proven themselves over years of typesetting use.

Readability is paramount—the spaces between letters, words and lines of type all assist or inhibit comfortable legibility. As Jan Tschichold so wisely

13

STYLE 3—*All flush right*

CHAPTER ONE

Headline

The typeface chosen for a book is perhaps the most important aspect of the whole design. Each typeface will convey a particular mood to the writing, unconsciously supporting the feelings invoked by the words. In this computer age of thousands of typefaces produced by many manufacturers, with trendy new faces designed every day, those that reign have proven themselves over years of typesetting use.

Readability is paramount—the spaces between letters, words and lines of type all assist or inhibit comfortable legibility. As Jan Tschichold so wisely stated: "Perfect typography depends on perfect harmony between all of its elements." This harmony is achieved by careful observation of the parts *and* the whole. A book that is improperly set can annoy the reader, in turn destroying the author's intended message, but a well-designed page will invite your eyes to read without distraction.

The typeface chosen for a book is perhaps the most important aspect of the whole design. Each typeface will convey a particular mood to the writing, unconsciously supporting the feelings invoked by the words. In this computer age of thousands of typefaces produced by many manufacturers, with trendy new faces designed every day, those that reign have proven themselves over years of typesetting use.

Readability is paramount—the spaces between letters, words and lines of type all assist or inhibit comfortable legibility. As Jan Tschichold so wisely stated: "Perfect typography depends on

13

STYLE 4—*for 8½ x 11" books, two columns*

The Front Matter

It often helps to look at the front matter of books in the library and bookstores to get ideas. Some books require more formal and detailed front matter depending upon the subject matter.

Following are the guidelines we use when formatting the front matter pages. Each book is different and not all of these pages are necessary in every book, but this order is the industry standard.

The headlines of these pages are usually about 4-8 points bigger than the text point size and should be designed differently than the chapter headlines. To further set them apart from the chapter headlines, they should start lower on the page, have wider or lesser space between the headline and text, or be set with a different left-to-right alignment.

Title Page

The Title page is the one page that creates a transition between the cover and the text pages. Since a decorative face is usually chosen for the book's cover, the title is often set in a smaller version of the cover type. The author's name can be set in the same face used on the cover, or the same face as the text face.

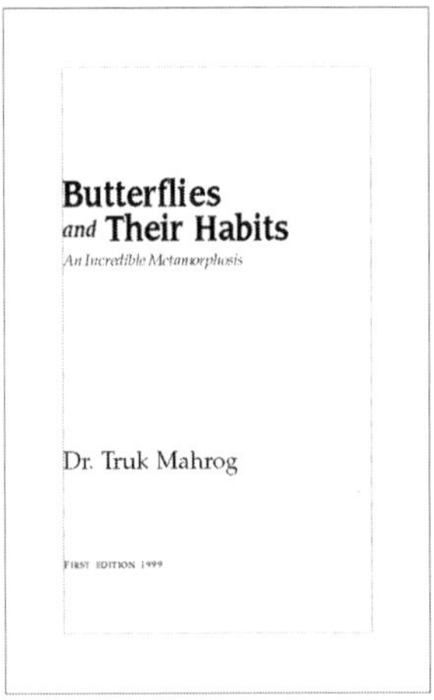

This page is always on the right-hand side. It may include a small piece of artwork relating to the cover, or a small graphical element between the title and author. A page number never appears on this page.

Copyright Page

This page is always on the left. The typesize is smaller than that used for the body of the text, but it is usually the same face. It can be set flush left, centered or flush right, depending upon how the rest of the book is set up. It is usually set up so the last line falls at the bottom margin boundary. A page number never appears on this page.

Dedication Page

The Dedication is usually across from the Copyright page. Often it is set in italics or with a decorative first letter of script or italics (a simulation of handwriting, an implication to the reader that this is a personal note from the author). It is usually set a few points bigger than the point size of the body text. Again, it should follow the format of the rest of the book and be aligned

If you will be submitting your book to the copyright office, the copyright page must contain the © symbol or the word "copyright" followed by the year printed and the name of the author. After this, include a generic wording such as "All rights reserved"; there are many variations. Optional information to include on this page are: the ISBN, the Library of Congress Control Number and the CIP data.

> The standards and conventions of setting up what belongs on a right hand or left hand page are only that—standards and conventions. There are many instances in which these standards may not be applicable or desirable. First and foremost, it is your book and it should look the way you desire.

either centered, flush-right or flush-left. It is usually set either in the middle of the page, or approximately three inches from the top page boundary to distinguish it from the tops of the text pages. It is often unnecessary to have the word "Dedication" on top, because the text usually is worded in such a way for that to be redundant (i.e.: *I dedicate this book to my mother…)*.

Foreword

A Foreword is generally written about the book by someone other than the author and is usually about 2-4 pages long. If there is a Foreword, it should appear on the next available right-hand page after the Dedication, and the left-hand page should be blank.

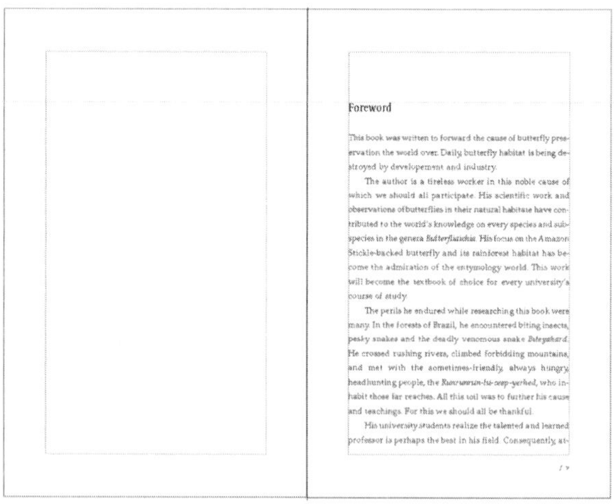

Contents

The words "Table of Contents" have gone out of favor in recent years; "Contents" is deemed sufficient. Almost all books contain a Contents page, however, some do not. If you decide to have a Contents page, all sections and chapters should be included, plus subheadlines if it is a technical work. It should start at the top of the page in the same location as the rest of the front matter with a similarly designed headline. When designing this page avoid using a line of dots between the chapter and its corresponding page number. It is better to place the number just before the chapter name or just after.

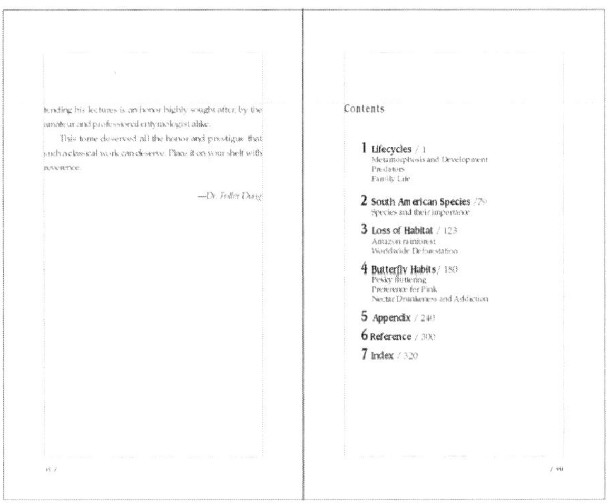

Preface

The Preface is written by the author and contains the reasons for writing the book and the research undertaken. If there is a Preface, it should appear on the next available right-hand page after the Contents, and the left-hand page should be blank or include the end of the Contents.

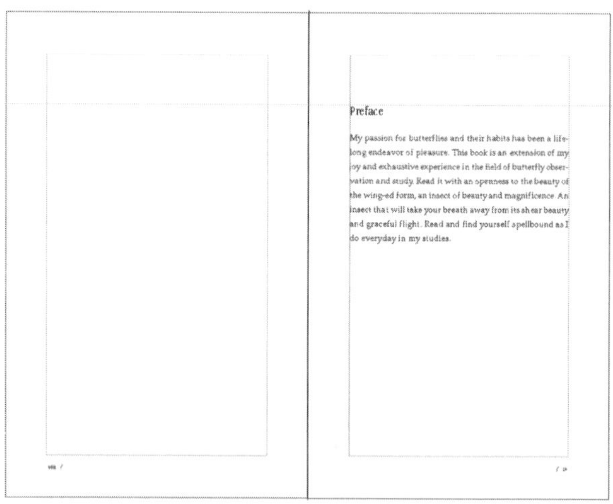
Preface

My passion for butterflies and their habits has been a lifelong endeavor of pleasure. This book is an extension of my joy and exhaustive experience in the field of butterfly observation and study. Read it with an openness to the beauty of the wing-ed form, an insect of beauty and magnificence. An insect that will take your breath away from its shear beauty and graceful flight. Read and find yourself spellbound as I do everyday in my studies.

Acknowledgments

The Acknowledgments page is the author's area to thank all those people who assisted in any phases of the book's production. It should appear on the next available right-hand page after the Preface, and the left-hand page should be blank or include the end of the Preface.

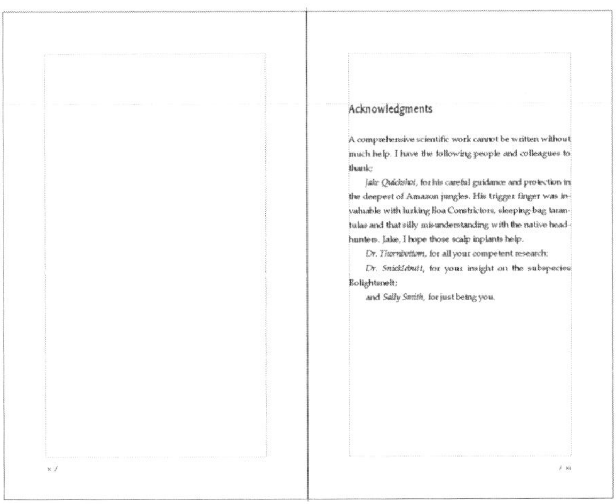

Acknowledgments

A comprehensive scientific work cannot be written without much help. I have the following people and colleagues to thank:

Jake Quickshot, for his careful guidance and protection in the deepest of Amazon jungles. His trigger finger was invaluable with lurking Boa Constrictors, sleeping-bag tarantulas and that silly misunderstanding with the native headhunters. Jake, I hope those scalp inplants help.

Dr. Thornbottom, for all your competent research;

Dr. Snicklebutt, for your insight on the subspecies Bolightsnelt;

and *Sally Smith*, for just being you.

The front matter pages usually start lower down on the page than the first pages of the chapters. The Dedication, Foreword, Contents, Preface, Acknowledgments and Introduction all start consistently at the same location on the page. The two exceptions are: the title page which is placed on the page wherever it looks most balanced and the copyright page, where the text is placed to line up at the bottom.

Front matter is often not included in the page numbering of a book. Often Page 1 will start on the first page of chapter one. If there are many pages of front matter, they are often numbered separately using lowercase Roman numerals.

Introduction

The introduction contains material relevant to the text and should be read before the rest of the book, for example, the historical background for the book. It should appear just before the first chapter, and should start on a right-hand page.

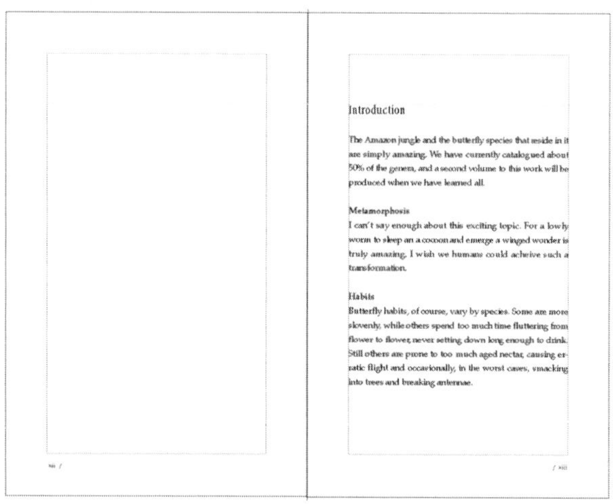

The Back Matter

Not all books require all of these pages, but this order is the industry standard.

Appendix

The appendix usually contains explanations that help clarify the text, such as laws, documents, lists, charts and tables.

Notes

When a notation or explanation is too large for a footnote, it should go in this section.

Glossary

An alphabetical glossary is useful in a technical work with complicated terms that require explanation.

Bibliography

There are many ways to set up a bibliography, depending on the style of the book or how many sources were used. Check the *Chicago Manual of Style* for specific information.

Index

Indexing is time-consuming and is best done by hand as the book is being written. The page numbers can be added after the book is formatted.

Order Form

This page is usually set on the book's last right-hand page with a blank back-side so the reader can cut or tear it out if necessary. It should be clear and concise.

The back matter type size is sometimes smaller than the rest of the body text since it is used for reference. The headlines for back matter should be set in the same manner as the front matter and start in the same location on the page.

APPENDICES

Submitting
book materials,
Information on type,
Marketing
your book

APPENDIX A Submitting book materials

If your book will be designed by Gorham Printing

Text

To design your text pages, we will need to have a raw text file of the book to import into a page layout program (PageMaker or InDesign). You can type your book in just about any wordprocessing program, PC or Mac. Some programs we can accept:

- Microsoft Word (any version)
- Wordperfect
- Microsoft Publisher

Please call us if you are using an older version or lesser known software program. We will likely be able to make it work, however, please check. It is best to have the whole book saved as a single file, with no graphics or photos included—we will add those later.

Photos
For the best printed results, we recommend that you have us scan and prepare your photographs. However, if you have already scanned the photos or graphics for the text, it is important that no graphics or photos be placed into your text file; but be separate files. For us to readily determine where you wish us to place a photo, simply hit return, then designate "photo (number) here", hit return again and continue with the manuscript.

Cover

To design the cover for your book, we usually take a combination of your cover ideas, pictures and the content of the book to determine the best look for your cover. We have designed covers of every subject and style, so we are adept at creating just the right look for you. We will send you proofs as we go along, for you to approve, correct and adjust.

How many pages?

When we import your file into our page layout program, and design the text, the number of pages will probably change from the original document. To get an idea of the final page count, use the following formula: For a 5½ x 8½″ size book, figure approximately 300 words per page and for a 6 x 9″ size book figure approximately 350 words per page. For example, if your book contained 48,000 words, it would end up at approximately 160 total pages for a 5½ x 8½″ size book. (48,000 words ÷ 300 words per page = 160 5½ x 8½″ finished pages).

A few things to consider: If you have photos or drawings, don't forget to include them in your page count. If your book has short chapters, the page count will also likely go up. We will most likely get more words to the page than the word count used in the formula, but when figuring chapter headings, front matter, back matter, etc. the formula is a fairly accurate average page counter.

Photo Tips

- The quality of the printed photo will depend upon the quality of the original. We can do minor repairs to photos, but if they are blurry or seriously damaged, we will not be able to achieve a quality outcome.
- Good quality color photos can be easily reproduced as black and white. Photos can also be reduced and enlarged as needed.
- Halftones made from previously printed photos also give marginal results. (Remember to check copyright restrictions.)

If you are providing your book on disk ready for trouble-free output

A Word about Word
Many authors use Microsoft Word to type the manuscript of their book. Native Word files (.doc files) however, can create technical problems when printed to our imagesetter, so we are unable to accept them as is. You have options at this point.

• We can design the layout of your book

• You can do the layout and design yourself, without incurring additional charges, and send us a .pdf or postscript file.

See our website for more detailed information.

Text

The best way to send us the text of your book, is as a .pdf file. While it usually requires that you purchase a program, Acrobat Distiller, we have found that it will often save you money in the long run because you will have little or no troubleshooting costs to your file. It also guarantees that what you see on screen and print on your printer, is what we see and print.

We can accept native files in any of the following PC-platform software:

- PageMaker 6.0–7.0
- Quark XPress 4.0
- Adobe InDesign 1.0–2.0
- Microsoft Publisher 2000 or newer

Cover

We can accept native files in any of the following PC-platform software:

- PageMaker 6.0–7.0
- Quark XPress 4.0
- Adobe InDesign 1.0–2.0
- Adobe Illustrator 10 or earlier
- Macromedia Freehand 8.0
- Microsoft Publisher 2000 or newer

We can also accept covers as a .pdf or created with Mac software, as long as we can switch the fonts over to PC (this would be done at extra cost). We can also accept .eps or .prn files, but you would need to be sure that every element is "in stone" before sending to us; as changes cannot be made.

Fonts

You will need to send us *every* instance of every font used on your text pages and cover. If you will be sending an .eps file, you will need to embed fonts, or convert any fonts to outlines that will not embed.

Linking photos and graphics

If you will not be sending a .pdf, you must have all graphics linked to the file—*not embedded*. Embedded graphics result in huge files that are sometimes impossible to output to our imagesetter correctly.

More detailed information is available on our website.

Spine

If the spine of your book will be any small than 3/8″ wide, all spine type should be All Caps, and allow for 1/16″ space to either side of the words. It is vitally important that the spine width be set correctly for the amount of pages in your book and the type of paper.

APPENDIX B Information on Type

Designing the Body Text

Book design (or typesetting) does not follow the same rules that are taught in a traditional typing class. When setting up text pages, the following guidelines will help you in producing professional-looking pages.

1. Book text is usually *justified*, spanning the width of the text column between the margins. For example, the opposite page is justified and this list is flush left.

2. Italics should be used for emphasis. Avoid using all caps, underlining or bold type.

3. Books are often set somewhat smaller than 12 points. Open some of your own books that you enjoy reading and you will probably be surprised at the size of the type.

4. Use indents at the beginning of each paragraph rather than gaps or open areas between paragraphs. Indents should be small (.25 of an inch).

5. Only use one space after periods for ease in justification.

DEFINITION

Point Size
The unit of measure for the size of letters. There are 12 points in one pica and 6 picas in one inch.

Leading
The space between lines of type.

Samples of Body Text

The typeface chosen for the body text (the main story of the book) is particularly important to the book's overall mood. For example, an instructive manual on engineering might be best set in a blocky, vertical face with an angular feeling; but a romance novel might have a flowery, round typeface with an attractive set of italics. The reader will probably never really look directly at each letter of the typeface, but its mood will be conveyed subconsciously.

The following pages include six of our most-often-used typefaces set as body text. The space between the letters and words has been fine-tuned, as has the type size in relation to the space between the lines (leading). There are three sets for each typeface. You may use these charts to figure an approximate page count for your book.

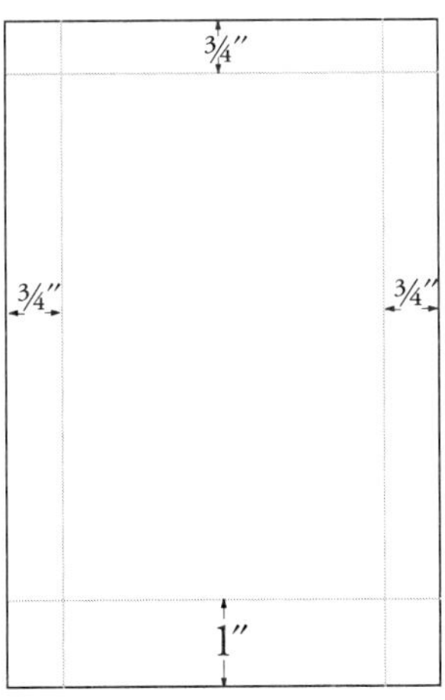

The margins at left are used for both 6 x 9 ″ and 5½ x 8½ ″ books.

You can use the samples on the next 10 pages to approximate how many pages your book will have based on the final size and the total word count.

Bembo is arguably the most readable typeface of all and works in any type of book. Derived from the Aldus typeface of the Renaissance, it is proportioned well and is quiet and simple.

Bembo

REGULAR

ABCDEFGHIJKLMNOPQRSTUVWXYZ
abcdefghijklmnopqrstuvwxyz
1234567890 ½&;!?"

ITALICS

ABCDEFGHIJKLMNOPQRSTUVWXYZ
abcdefghijklmnopqrstuvwxyz
1234567890 ½&;!?"

BOLD

ABCDEFGHIJKLMNOPQRSTUVWXYZ
abcdefghijklmnopqrstuvwxyz
1234567890 ½&;!?"

BOLD ITALICS

ABCDEFGHIJKLMNOPQRSTUVWXYZ
abcdefghijklmnopqrstuvwxyz
1234567890 ½&;!?"

10.5 POINT TYPE / 14 POINT LEADING

The typeface chosen for a book is perhaps the most important aspect of the whole design. Each typeface will convey a particular mood to the writing, subconsciously supporting the feelings evoked by the words. In this computer age of thousands of typefaces produced by many manufacturers, with trendy new faces designed every day, those that reign have proven themselves over years of typesetting use.

Readability is paramount—the spaces between letters,

SPACE SAVER:

5½ x 8½″: 350 words/page

6 x 9″: 450 words/page

11 POINT TYPE / 14.5 POINT LEADING

The typeface chosen for a book is perhaps the most important aspect of the whole design. Each typeface will convey a particular mood to the writing, subconsciously supporting the feelings evoked by the words. In this computer age of thousands of typefaces produced by many manufacturers, with trendy new faces designed every day, those that reign have proven themselves over years of typesetting use.

Readability is paramount—the spaces between letters, words and lines of type all assist or inhibit

OPTIMUM:

5½ x 8½″: 315 words/page

6 x 9″: 420 words/page

11.5 POINT TYPE / 16 POINT LEADING

The typeface chosen for a book is perhaps the most important aspect of the whole design. Each typeface will convey a particular mood to the writing, subconsciously supporting the feelings evoked by the words. In this computer age of thousands of typefaces produced by many manufacturers, with trendy new faces designed every day, those that reign have proven themselves over years of typesetting use.

Readability is paramount—the spaces between let-

LARGE TYPE:

5½ x 8½″: 280 words/page

6 x 9″: 320 words/page

Garamond was designed in the 1500s, but it has a timeless appeal. The letterforms are open and round, resulting in a highly readable typeface. It has a soft feeling, and is well-suited to poetry books and novels.

Garamond

REGULAR

ABCDEFGHIJKLMNOPQRSTUVWXYZ
abcdefghijklmnopqrstuvwxyz
1234567890 ½&;!?"

ITALIC

ABCDEFGHIJKLMNOPQRSTUVWXYZ
abcdefghijklmnopqrstuvwxyz
1234567890 ½&;!?"

BOLD

ABCDEFGHIJKLMNOPQRSTUVWXYZ
abcdefghijklmnopqrstuvwxyz
1234567890 ½&;!?"

BOLD ITALIC

ABCDEFGHIJKLMNOPQRSTUVWXYZ
abcdefghijklmnopqrstuvwxyz
1234567890 ½&;!?"

10.5 POINT TYPE / 14 POINT LEADING

The typeface chosen for a book is perhaps the most important aspect of the whole design. Each typeface will convey a particular mood to the writing, subconsciously supporting the feelings evoked by the words. In this computer age of thousands of typefaces produced by many manufacturers, with trendy new faces designed every day, those that reign have proven themselves over years of typesetting use.

Readability is paramount—the spaces between let-

SPACE SAVER:
5½ x 8½″: 420 words/page
6 x 9″: 490 words/page

11 POINT TYPE / 14.5 POINT LEADING

The typeface chosen for a book is perhaps the most important aspect of the whole design. Each typeface will convey a particular mood to the writing, subconsciously supporting the feelings evoked by the words. In this computer age of thousands of typefaces produced by many manufacturers, with trendy new faces designed every day, those that reign have proven themselves over years of typesetting use.

Readability is paramount—the spaces between letters, words and lines of type all assist or inhibit comfort-

OPTIMUM:
5½ x 8½″: 380 words/page
6 x 9″: 460 words/page

11.5 POINT TYPE / 16 POINT LEADING

The typeface chosen for a book is perhaps the most important aspect of the whole design. Each typeface will convey a particular mood to the writing, subconsciously supporting the feelings evoked by the words. In this computer age of thousands of typefaces produced by many manufacturers, with trendy new faces designed every day, those that reign have proven themselves over years of typesetting use.

Readability is paramount—the spaces between let-

LARGE TYPE:
5½ x 8½″: 340 words/page
6 x 9″: 390 words/page

Minion

Minion is a very modern typeface, designed by Robert Slimbach in 1990 and inspired by classical Renaissance typefaces. It is very readable and applicable for any style of book.

REGULAR

ABCDEFGHIJKLMNOPQRSTUVWXYZ
abcdefghijklmnopqrstuvwxyz
1234567890 ½&;!?"

ITALIC

ABCDEFGHIJKLMNOPQRSTUVWXYZ
abcdefghijklmnopqrstuvwxyz
1234567890 ½&;!?"

BOLD

ABCDEFGHIJKLMNOPQRSTUVWXYZ
abcdefghijklmnopqrstuvwxyz
1234567890 ½&;!?"

BOLD ITALIC

ABCDEFGHIJKLMNOPQRSTUVWXYZ
abcdefghijklmnopqrstuvwxyz
1234567890 ½&;!?"

10 POINT TYPE / 14 POINT LEADING

The typeface chosen for a book is perhaps the most important aspect of the whole design. Each typeface will convey a particular mood to the writing, subconsciously supporting the feelings evoked by the words. In this computer age of thousands of typefaces produced by many manufacturers, with trendy new faces designed every day, those that reign have proven themselves over years of typesetting use.

Readability is paramount—the spaces between letters, words and lines of type all assist or inhibit comfortable

SPACE SAVER:
5½ x 8½″: 360 words/page
6 x 9″: 429 words/page

11 POINT TYPE / 16 POINT LEADING

The typeface chosen for a book is perhaps the most important aspect of the whole design. Each typeface will convey a particular mood to the writing, subconsciously supporting the feelings evoked by the words. In this computer age of thousands of typefaces produced by many manufacturers, with trendy new faces designed every day, those that reign have proven themselves over years of typesetting use.

Readability is paramount—the spaces between letters, words and lines of type all assist or inhibit

OPTIMUM:
5½ x 8½″: 315 words/page
6 x 9″: 410 words/page

11.5 POINT TYPE / 16.5 POINT LEADING

The typeface chosen for a book is perhaps the most important aspect of the whole design. Each typeface will convey a particular mood to the writing, subconsciously supporting the feelings evoked by the words. In this computer age of thousands of typefaces produced by many manufacturers, with trendy new faces designed every day, those that reign have proven themselves over years of typesetting use.

Readability is paramount—the spaces between letters, words and lines of type all assist or inhibit

LARGE TYPE:
5½ x 8½″: 280 words/page
6 x 9″: 380 words/page

Palatino was designed in the 1950s in Germany, and is a popular modern typeface. It has a rather angular appearance and exudes a feeling of strength. It has a particularly beautiful set of calligraphic italics.

Palatino

REGULAR

ABCDEFGHIJKLMNOPQRSTUVWXYZ
abcdefghijklmnopqrstuvwxyz
1234567890 ½&;!?"

ITALIC

ABCDEFGHIJKLMNOPQRSTUVWXYZ
abcdefghijklmnopqrstuvwxyz
1234567890 ½&;!?"

BOLD

ABCDEFGHIJKLMNOPQRSTUVWXYZ
abcdefghijklmnopqrstuvwxyz
1234567890 ½&;!?"

BOLD ITALIC

ABCDEFGHIJKLMNOPQRSTUVWXYZ
abcdefghijklmnopqrstuvwxyz
1234567890 ½&;!?"

9 POINT TYPE / 13 POINT LEADING

The typeface chosen for a book is perhaps the most important aspect of the whole design. Each typeface will convey a particular mood to the writing, subconsciously supporting the feelings evoked by the words. In this computer age of thousands of typefaces produced by many manufacturers, with trendy new faces designed every day, those that reign have proven themselves over years of typesetting use.

Readability is paramount—the spaces between letters, words and lines of type all assist or inhibit comfortable

SPACE SAVER:
5½ x 8½″: 450 words/page
6 x 9″: 510 words/page

10 POINT TYPE / 14 POINT LEADING

The typeface chosen for a book is perhaps the most important aspect of the whole design. Each typeface will convey a particular mood to the writing, subconsciously supporting the feelings evoked by the words. In this computer age of thousands of typefaces produced by many manufacturers, with trendy new faces designed every day, those that reign have proven themselves over years of typesetting use.

Readability is paramount—the spaces between letters, words and lines of type all assist or inhibit

OPTIMUM:
5½ x 8½″: 380 words/page
6 x 9″: 450 words/page

10.8 POINT TYPE / 15 POINT LEADING

The typeface chosen for a book is perhaps the most important aspect of the whole design. Each typeface will convey a particular mood to the writing, subconsciously supporting the feelings evoked by the words. In this computer age of thousands of typefaces produced by many manufacturers, with trendy new faces designed every day, those that reign have proven themselves over years of typesetting use.

Readability is paramount—the spaces between

LARGE TYPE:
5½ x 8½″: 340 words/page
6 x 9″: 390 words/page

Times was designed in the 1930s in England for use in newspapers. Its narrow design was especially suited for the narrow columns of a newspaper and even in books it is the best typeface to conserve space. It is probably the most widely used typeface today, available on every computer and the Internet. There are many versions of this typeface.

Times

REGULAR

ABCDEFGHIJKLMNOPQRSTUVWXYZ
abcdefghijklmnopqrstuvwxyz
1234567890 ½&;!?"

ITALIC

ABCDEFGHIJKLMNOPQRSTUVWXYZ
abcdefghijklmnopqrstuvwxyz
1234567890 ½&;!?"

BOLD

ABCDEFGHIJKLMNOPQRSTUVWXYZ
abcdefghijklmnopqrstuvwxyz
1234567890 ½&;!?"

BOLD ITALIC

ABCDEFGHIJKLMNOPQRSTUVWXYZ
abcdefghijklmnopqrstuvwxyz
1234567890 ½&;!?"

10 POINT TYPE / 14 POINT LEADING

The typeface chosen for a book is perhaps the most important aspect of the whole design. Each typeface will convey a particular mood to the writing, subconsciously supporting the feelings evoked by the words. In this computer age of thousands of typefaces produced by many manufacturers, with trendy new faces designed every day, those that reign have proven themselves over years of typesetting use.

Readability is paramount—the spaces between letters, words and lines of type all assist or inhibit comfortable leg-

SPACE SAVER:
5½ x 8½″: 420 words/page
6 x 9″: 490 words/page

11 POINT TYPE / 15 POINT LEADING

The typeface chosen for a book is perhaps the most important aspect of the whole design. Each typeface will convey a particular mood to the writing, subconsciously supporting the feelings evoked by the words. In this computer age of thousands of typefaces produced by many manufacturers, with trendy new faces designed every day, those that reign have proven themselves over years of typesetting use.

Readability is paramount—the spaces between letters, words and lines of type all assist or inhibit

OPTIMUM:
5½ x 8½″: 360 words/page
6 x 9″: 425 words/page

11.5 POINT TYPE / 16 POINT LEADING

The typeface chosen for a book is perhaps the most important aspect of the whole design. Each typeface will convey a particular mood to the writing, subconsciously supporting the feelings evoked by the words. In this computer age of thousands of typefaces produced by many manufacturers, with trendy new faces designed every day, those that reign have proven themselves over years of typesetting use.

Readability is paramount—the spaces between

LARGE TYPE:
5½ x 8½″: 310 words/page
6 x 9″: 400 words/page

APPENDIX C Marketing your book

Marketing an unknown book by an unknown author can be a challenge, to say the least. Self-publishers generally do not have the contacts or the clout to maneuver their books into the major book selling avenues. Another stumbling block is quantity vs. cost. Printing 1,000 books is considerably more expensive per book than printing 10,000 books. Therefore, there is less profit in selling books from a short run. Gambling on being able to sell 10,000 may not be a good bet either. The general consensus seems to be to print a smaller quantity and hope to break even, and then go into a second printing if warranted. A second printing is less expensive because most of the setup costs have already been paid.

Targeting your audience will help you in your marketing efforts. Consider who your readers will be, how many there are and where they are located. It is often helpful to talk to bookstore owners about your project. They may be interested in handling your book and have insights about potential markets.

Some authors deal with subject matter that has a small field of interest. These books are sometimes easier to sell because it is easier to identify the market. For example, a book on rock hunting in Western Washington might be promoted with greater success by sending out flyers to rock clubs than by trying to work through a mass market bookstore.

Over the years, we have talked to many authors about their self-marketing efforts. The following pages list some techniques they have found helpful.

BEFORE THE BOOK IS SUBMITTED FOR PRINTING

Apply for ISBN and/or LCCN-(See pages 23 and 24.) Processing can take be ten days to two weeks.

Consult a professional editor-to help polish your book.

Create a logo-of your own company or a logo simply using the title of your book, in the same design as the cover. Place on all correspondence and publications for marketing your book.

DURING THE DESIGN PHASE

The back cover-Your back cover should include the subject category at the top, this will help bookstores know where to place it on their shelves. Also include a concise explanation of what is inside the book.

An order form-Placed on one of the last pages, the order form is an excellent way to maintain continuing sales of the book.

WHILE THE BOOK IS IN PRODUCTION

Get a website-Obtain a domain name for your company or book title. Have a website created that showcases information about your book, including excerpts, an image of your book cover and a way for book orders to be submitted to you via the web.

Create promotional pieces-have a professional designer create items to assist in marketing; such as bookmarks with your web address or phone number, posters, fliers, brochures or extra printed covers.

> Check out regional and national booksellers and small publishing groups for help in marketing.

You may want to consider marketing avenues long before your book is printed as an aid to determining quantities to have printed.

Arrange to use a distributor-Many bookstores prefer to buy their books from distributors such as Ingram or Baker & Taylor. A distributor handles your book for a fee (usually 50-60%).

Approach stores-Approach locally-owned bookstores or other retail outlets and get your books into as many of them as possible. Even if they require a 40 to 60% cut, the exposure is important.

Approach online bookstores or retailers-Sites like *Amazon.com* and *Barnes&Noble.com* make it easy for customers to find and purchase your book.

AFTER THE BOOKS ARE PRINTED

Create an email announcement-A simple email letter with an image of your book cover can help you spread the word about your book.

Contact newspapers, magazines or local radio and television-To promote your book, make yourself available for interviews or book reviews. Try specialized publications that apply specifically to your title.

Host an autograph party. Send out invitations and flyers in advance to advertise the release of your book.

Arrange speaking engagements-Offer to speak for free as an expert in your field and subject matter, and sell your book afterward.

Enter writing or design competitions. Many organizations sponsor awards for excellence in writing.

GLOSSARY

back matter—The pages after the main text of the book that contain the reference matter, including: Appendix(es), Notes, Glossary, Bibliography, List of Contributors, Index(es) and Order Form (most often in that order).

bleed—A printed image that extends "off the page" is known as a bleed.

body text—The main text body of the book, separate from the display type such as headlines, subheadlines, chapter openings, etc.

CMYK—Initials designating Cyan (C), Magenta (M), Yellow (Y) and Black (K). Also known as the four process colors.

color separations—The conversion of a color photograph or drawing into its component spectral colors: Cyan, Yellow, Magenta and Black (CMYK) with one screened negative produced per color.

copyright—A book is copyrighted when the author's name, date of copyright and the copyright symbol (©) or the word "copyright" appear on the copyright page (usually the first left-hand page after the title page).

crop marks—Small lines on the outer edges of a book cover that indicate the final trim size after it is bound.

registration—To print an image in correct relation to other images already printed on the same sheet.

formatting—The process of importing a raw text file into a page-layout program and designing the final book pages.

four-color process (full color) printing—The process of using four colors to print a single image, resulting in an image that looks full color to the naked eye. The ink colors used are: Cyan, Magenta, Yellow and Black.

front matter—The pages before the main text of the book that contain the Title page, Copyright page, Dedication, Foreword, Contents, Preface, Acknowledgment and Introduction (most often in that order.)

halftone—A process whereby a photograph is broken up into a pattern of dots of varying size from which a printing plate is made. When printed, the dots of the image merge to the naked eye to give the impression of shades of gray.

header—Headers appear at the top of each page in the book (except chapter openings) and contain either the author name, book name or chapter name. They are designed to help the reader navigate around the book.

imagesetter—A machine that digitally images computer files onto light-sensitive film negatives, at a high resolution. The printing plates are made from shining light through the film negatives.

ISBN—International Standard Book Number. A registration number obtained from R. R. Bowker that is used by bookstores to track and obtain titles.

Library of Congress Control Number—A registration number obtained from the Library of Congress and is used to distribute books intended for libraries.

leading—The space between lines of type.

OCR scanning—Optical Character Recognition is the process of translating typed or printed characters into digital form. The text is saved as if it were originally typed, not as an image.

offset printing—The transfer of an inked image to paper through an intermediate, or blanket, cylinder.

on-line—Accessing an Internet address through the use of a computer and modem.

negative (film)—A photographic image in which light values are reversed. Light is passed through this image onto a light-sensitive printing plate which is used on the press.

publishing (traditional)—Books that are printed, marketed and distributed by a publishers are said to be *published.* Writers receive a share of the profits. *See self-publishing.*

resolution—The quality of a digital output, as defined by the number of dots (pixels) per inch. The higher the number, the higher the quality.

sans-serif—A typeface without serifs (the short lines projecting from the top or bottom of the main stroke of a letter). *See serif.*

self-publishing—When an author chooses to print, market and distribute a book, paying all costs and keeping all rights and profits.

serif—The short lines that project from the top or bottom of the main stroke of a letter. *See sans-serif.*

signature—Folded book pages that are usually in groups of 8, 16 or 32. In the case of a 16–page signature, 8 pages are printed on each side of a large sheet of paper. The sheet is then folded into a signature. The signatures are bound together at the spine.

smyth sewn—A binding with threads sewn through the back fold of the signature, with threads carried also from signature to signature, linking them together, while permitting complete opening of the book to the back.

spine—The back of the book where the bound pages come together. Also the part of the book that is visible on bookshelves.

trapping—To anticipate mis-registration on the press that might result in an unintended white space where two printed colors are next to one another. One of the ink colors is made bigger (spread) or smaller (choke) to compensate for variables in printing.

trim size—The dimensions of the finished book, after it is printed, bound and trimmed on three sides.

A GUIDE TO BOOK PRINTING & SELF-PUBLISHING
has been typeset and printed
by Gorham Printing of Rochester, Washington.

The book was designed by Kathy Campbell using Adobe Garamond.
Printing by Del Burd. Bindery by Dan Koivula

The text pages are printed on 60 lb. white Georgia Pacific Spectrum offset paper.
The cover is printed on white 10 point coated stock, with gloss lamination.